Contents

Macmillan Education
4 Crinan Street
London N1 9XW
A division of Macmillan Education Limited

Companies and representatives throughout the world

Ferris Wheel Level 1 Student's Book ISBN 978-1-380-01866-3
Ferris Wheel Level 1 Student's Book with Navio App ISBN 978-1-380-02660-6

First published 2019

Original design by Clare Webber
Page make-up by emc design ltd.
Illustrated by Animation Group Sp. z.o.o. based on original character design by Jose Ignacio Gómez (Nacho Gómez)
Cover design by emc design ltd
Cover illustration by Animation Group Sp. z.o.o. based on original character design by Jose Ignacio Gómez (Nacho Gómez)
Picture research by Lorraine Beck

Author's acknowledgements
I would like to thank everyone at Macmillan Education in the UK, Spain and Mexico who has contributed to the development and production of these materials. I would also like to thank all the teachers who have taken time to read and pilot the materials, and given invaluable feedback at every stage of writing the course. Special thanks as ever go to my husband, Alan, for his encouragement and support, and to our son and daughter, Jamie and Hannah, from whose early childhood days I learnt so much.

The publishers would like to thank Alex Tamulis, São Paulo, Brazil; Ayşegül Sezer, İNO Schools, Turkey; Daniela Araujo Pielli, Alt Idiomas, São Bernardo Do Campo, Brazil; Daniela Pugliese, Milton's College, Buenos Aires, Argentina; Esra Ezici, Turkey; Fernanda Domeniconi Nery Amorim, São Paulo, Brazil; Gabriela Iocolari, English Schoolhouse, Buenos Aires, Argentina; Gulbin Cin, Bahcesehir College, Turkey; Mariana Pastorino, Em Pi Instituto de Inglés, Santa Fe, Argentina; Mariné Ortiz, Warrington, Buenos Aires, Argentina; Paola Daniela Tuninetti, Academia Argüello, Córdoba, Argentina; Silvana Paola Accardo, Escuela Cooperativa Mundo Nuevo Instituto Casa de Jesús, Buenos Aires, Argentina.

The authors and publishers would like to thank the following for permission to reproduce their photographs:

Alamy Stock Photo/Michael Burrell pp15(eraser), 76(bucket), Alamy Stock Photo/Robert Hicks p15(pencil), Alamy Stock Photo/Martin Lee pp55, 59, 61(sandwich), Alamy Stock Photo/MBI p9(sister), Alamy Stock Photo/Pick and Mix Images p76(spade), Alamy Stock Photo/StockPhotosArt - Sweets pp55, 61(cookie), Alamy Stock Photo/Steve Taylor ARPS p81(crab), Alamy Stock Photo/Andrew Twort p35(hat), Alamy Stock Photo/SABAR UDIN pp75, 76(sea), Alamy Stock Photo/Wavebreak Media ltd pp5, 6(c, grandmother,grandfather), Alamy Stock Photo/Björn Wylezich p15(book); **Getty Images**/AlexStar pp24, 64(modelling clay), Getty Images/aopsan p34(paper plate), Getty Images/artisteer p65(mouse), Getty Images/aurigadesign p71(bl), Getty Images/bazilfoto pp65(bird), 69(r), Getty Images/Corvalol pp55, 61(apple), Getty Images/cynoclub p69(mr), Getty Images/Davies and Starr pp75, 76(crab), Getty Images/Dorling Kindersley p35(tshirt), Getty Images/Eliza317 pp59, 61(water), Getty Images/EyeEm/Cristina Catlin p25(eye), Getty Images/EyeEm/Massimiliano Clari p66(cat), Getty Images/EyeEm/Frank Mcclintock p71(tl), Getty Images/EyeEm/Iain Mcconnell p81(cat), Getty Images/Aaron Foster p81(sea), Getty Images/GlobalP p65(rabbit), Getty Images/Alexandra Grablewski p9(brother), Getty Images/harmpeti pp55, 59, 61(banana), Getty Images/heinteh p35(shorts), Getty Images/Image Source p51(br), Getty Images/iStockphoto p25(mouth), Getty Images/Ivan-balvan p35(shoes), Getty Images/jskiba pp75, 76(shell), Getty Images/kbwills pp59, 61(juice), Getty Images/kickers p25(nose), Getty Images/Dave King p65(fish), Getty Images/lucielang p15(crayon), Getty Images/A. Martin UW Photography p81(fish), Getty Images/Microzoa p81(sea), Getty Images/parinyabinsuk p14(pegs), Getty Images/Jose Luis Pelaez Inc p9(grandmother,grandfather), Getty Images/photovideostock pp75, 76(sand), Getty Images/Ridofranz p9(father), Getty Images/Kinzie Riehm p51(tr), Getty Images/Serg_Velusceac pp14, 24, 34, 44, 54, 64, 74, 84(paints), Getty Images/Techin24 p25(ear); **iStockphoto**/alex_kz pp14, 34, 44, 54, 74, 84(glue); **PHOTODISC** p66(dog); **Shutterstock**/Artazump81(garden), Shutterstock/Johannes Kornelius p69(fish); **Spectrecom** pp9(tr, mother), 12(tr), 19, 22(tr), 29(c,tr), 32(tr), 39, 42(tr), 49(t), 52(tr), 59(tr), 62(tr), 69, 72(tr), 79, 82(tr); **www.imagesource.com** pp14, 54(string).

Commissioned photography by Helen Marsden pp6(tr), 7(tl), 11, 14(tissue paper,wool,1,2,3), 16, 17(tl), 21, 22(tl), 24(1,2,3), 26, 27(tl), 31(ear, eye, boy, girl), 32(Sophie,Tom), 34(wool,1,2,3), 36, 37(tl), 41, 42(bl,bm,br), 44(tissue paper, 1,2,3), 45, 46, 47(tl), 49(scooter,teddy), 51(tl, bl), 54(tissue paper,coathanger,1,2,3), 56, 57(tl), 59(Sophie,Tom), 61(tr), 64(1,2,3), 66(c), 67(tl), 71(tr), 74(tissue paper,1,2,3), 76(c), 77(tl), 81(tr), 84(tissue paper,1,2,3).

Printed and bound in Uruguay

2024
33

Hello Welcome!

Listen, point and sing *Hello, hello, hello*. Stick the stickers of Mimi and Dylan.
Language: Mimi, Dylan; boy, girl; Hello, I'm (Mimi).

Listen, point and sing *Welcome to the Ferris Wheel!* Color the pod red. Say.

Language: Mommy, Daddy, Mimi, Dylan; Ferris Wheel; red

Family
The Ferris Wheel

Vocabulary

Lesson 1

1:16 hello 1:17

Listen, point and repeat. Listen and play. Stick the family stickers. Say.
Language: mommy, daddy, brother, sister; blue, green, red, yellow

Listen and find the new family members. Listen, point and sing *Where's your grandma?* Color the circle next to Grandpa red. Color the circle next to Grandma blue. Ask and say.
Language: mommy, daddy, grandma, grandpa, brother, sister; Where's your (grandma)? Here.

Lesson 3 Story

Watch. Listen to the story *The Ferris Wheel*. Color the character on the wheel with Zara Zebra. Stick the story sticker. Ask and say. **Language:** mommy, daddy, grandma, grandpa, brother, sister; Ferris Wheel; blue, orange, pink, yellow; Where's (Grandma)? Here.

Lesson 4

Story Song

Family

Watch. Listen, point and sing *The Ferris Wheel song*. Color the pod blue. Say.

Language: mommy, grandma, sister; Ferris Wheel; Here we go. Round and round.

1:22

hello

Lesson 5

Speaking

Life skills

Family

Watch. Listen and point. Follow and draw a path to connect the pictures in order. Trace around Mommy. Ask and say. Language: mommy, daddy, grandma, grandpa, brother, sister; Where's your (sister)? Here. This is my (mommy).

Values I love my family

Listen, point and sing *I love my family*. Color the frame red. Say.
Language: mommy, daddy, grandma, grandpa, brother, sister; I love my (mommy).

1:25

hello

SOCIAL AND EMOTIONAL LEARNING

Listen and point. Color the wheels. Say.
Language: round, wheel; This is (a wheel). Wheels go round and round.

Lesson 8

Culture

Family

Watch. Listen, point and sing *The wheels on the bus.* Color the circles under the family members in the song. Say. Language: mommy, daddy, brother, sister; bus, wheels; The wheels on the bus go round and round.

Listen, point and say. Color the pods to show the family members you know. Stick the star sticker. Ask and say. Language: mommy, daddy, grandma, grandpa, brother, sister; blue, green, orange, pink, red, yellow; Where's your (sister)? Here. This is my (brother).

Project

COOPERATIVE LEARNING

Choose a member of your family. Paint and decorate your picture. Make a family display. Ask and say. **Language:** mommy, daddy, grandma, grandpa, brother, sister; Where's your (grandpa)? Here. This is my (sister). I love my (daddy).

hello

Classroom

Mimi's first day at school

Listen, point and repeat. Listen and play. Stick the classroom object stickers. Say.

Language: book, crayon, eraser, pencil; blue, orange, pink, yellow

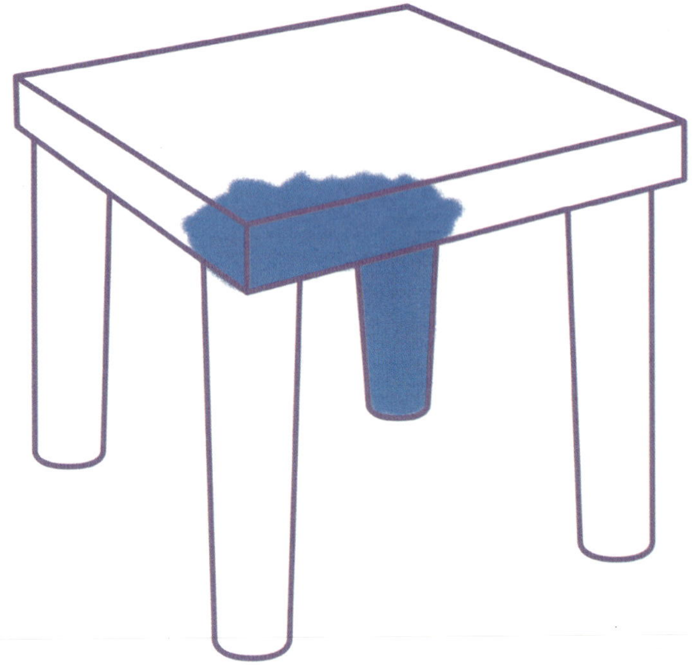

Listen and find the new classroom objects. Listen, point and sing *Stand up! Sit down!* Color the chair red and the table blue. Point and say. Language: book, chair, crayon, eraser, pencil, table; Sit down. Stand up. Look! It's (a chair).

Story

Watch. Listen to the story *Mimi's first day at school*. Color the characters who find the classroom objects. Stick the story sticker. Ask and say. Language: book, crayon, eraser, pencil; happy, sad; Look! It's (a crayon). Where's your (book)? Here. / I don't know. I'm (happy).

Story Song

Watch. Listen, point and sing *Where's your book?* Follow and draw the path through the maze. Ask and say. **Language:** book, crayon, eraser, pencil; happy, sad; Where's your (book)? Here. / I don't know. I'm (happy).

Classroom

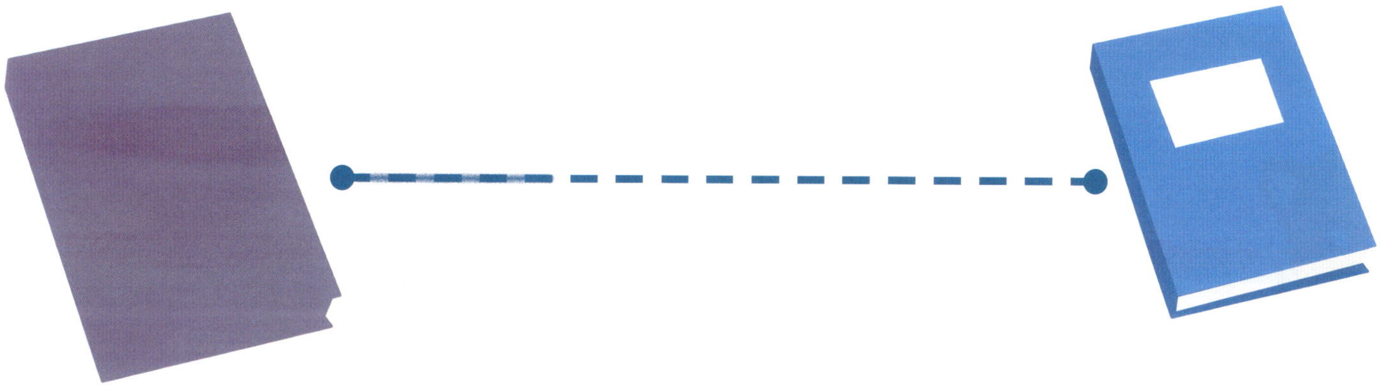

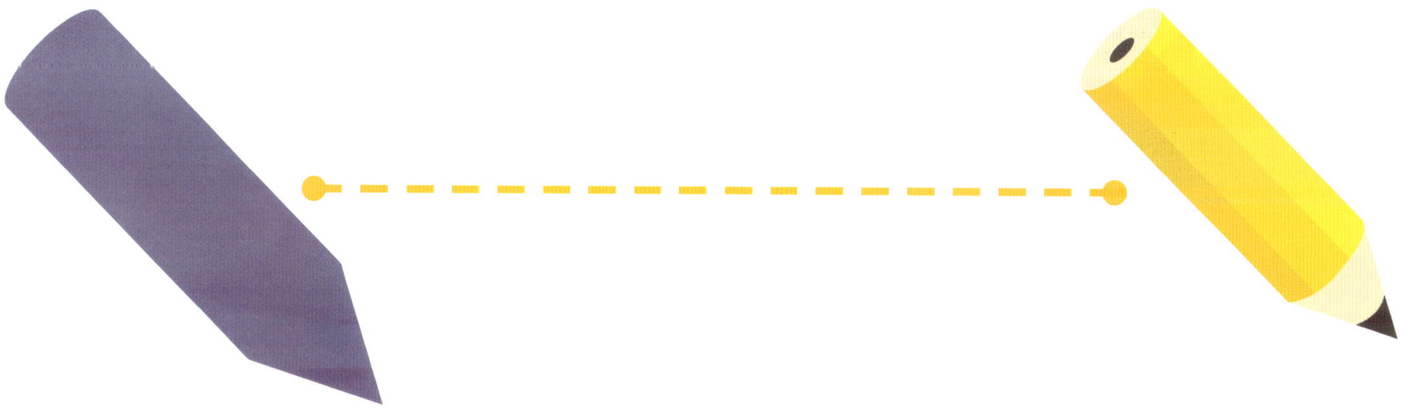

Watch. Listen and point. Trace to match the classroom objects. Ask and say. Language: book, pencil; blue, yellow; Where's your (book)? Here. What color is your (book)? It's (blue).

Lesson 8

Culture

Watch. Listen, point and sing *This is the way I say hello*. Follow and draw the path from Sophie and Tom to the school. Say.

Language: bye bye, hello; friends, school; This is the way I say (hello).

Review

Classroom

Listen, point and say. Color the words you know. Stick the star sticker. Ask and say. **Language:** book, chair, crayon, eraser, pencil, table; colors; It's (a crayon). Where's your (book)? Here. What color is your (book)? It's (blue).

COOPERATIVE LEARNING

1

2

3

Make some crayons and paint a tray. Put your crayons together in the trays. Ask and say.
Language: crayon, tray; colors; It's (a crayon). It's (red). Where's the (blue) crayon? Here.
What color is your (crayon)? It's (green). I put the crayon in the tray.

My face
Splash!

Listen, point and repeat. Listen and play. Stick the face stickers. Say.
Language: ear, eye, mouth, nose; blue, green, pink, red

Language

Listen and find the new parts of the face. Listen, point and sing *I have two eyes*. Trace to match Sophie's hair and Tom's teeth. Say. Language: ears, eyes, hair, mouth, nose, teeth; I have (a nose). I have (two) (eyes).

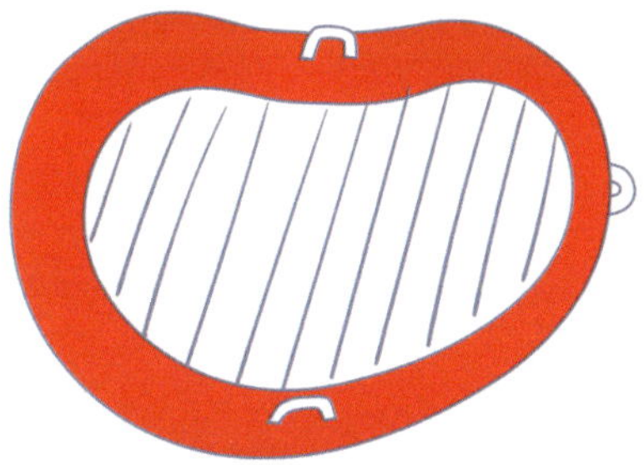

Watch. Listen to the story *Splash!* Color the boat from the story. Stick the story sticker. Say. Language: ears, eyes, mouth, nose; boy, girl; water; I have (a mouth).
I have (two) (eyes). It's (a boy) in the water.

Story Song

Watch. Listen, point and sing *Two eyes, two ears.* Follow and draw paths to match the pictures of Mimi and Dylan. Color the splashes in the water. Point and say.

Language: ears, eyes, mouth, nose; boy, girl; It's (a boy) in the water.

Life skills

My face

Watch. Listen and point. Color the puppet's eyes and nose.
Say. Language: ears, eyes, hair, mouth, nose; colors; I have (a red) (mouth). I have (two) (green) (ears).

Values I'm happy I'm me

My face

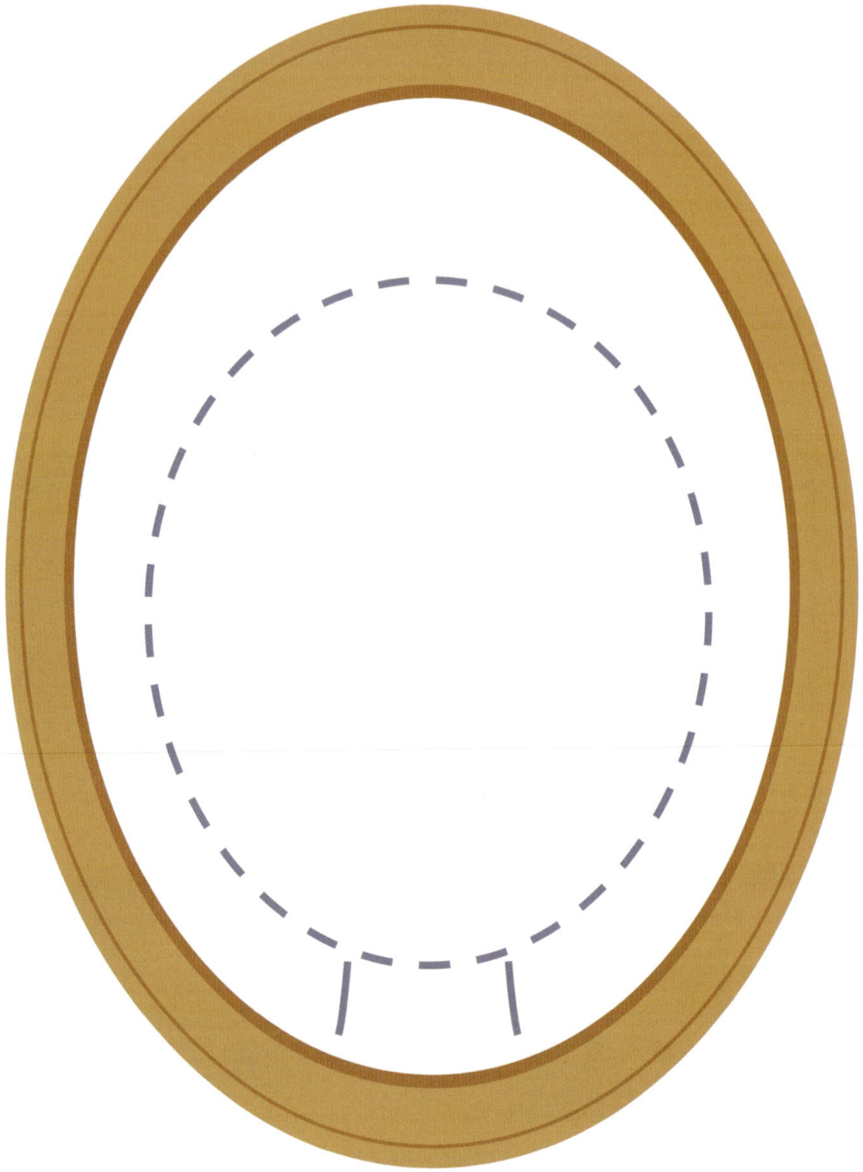

2:10

Listen, point and sing *I'm happy I'm me*. Trace and draw a picture of your face. Say. Language: ears, eyes, hair, mouth, nose, teeth; happy, special; My (eyes) are special.

SOCIAL AND EMOTIONAL LEARNING

Lesson 7 Content

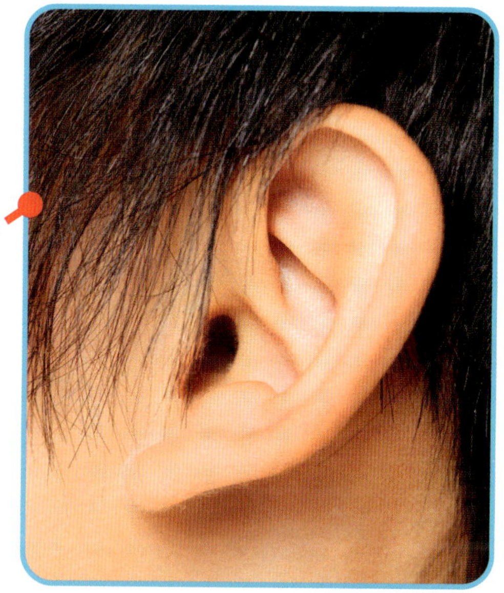

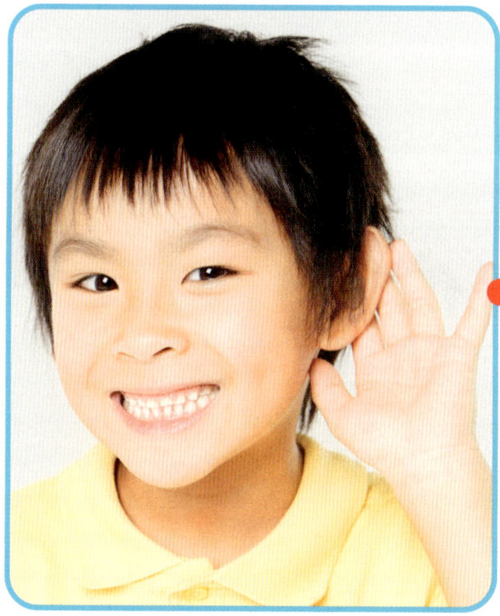

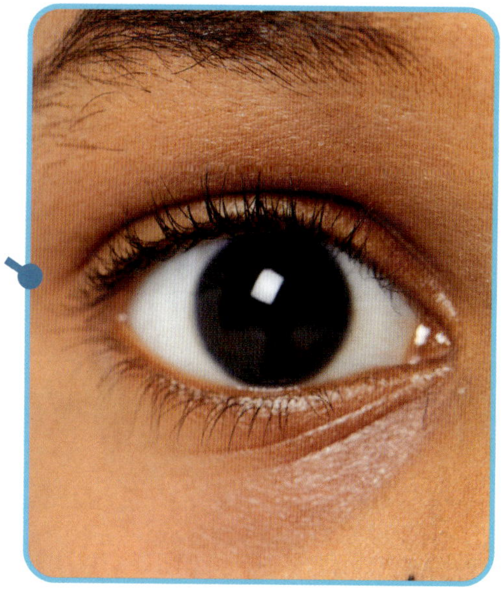

Listen and point. Trace to match the pictures. Say.
Language: hear, see; ears, eyes; I (see) with my (eyes).

Culture

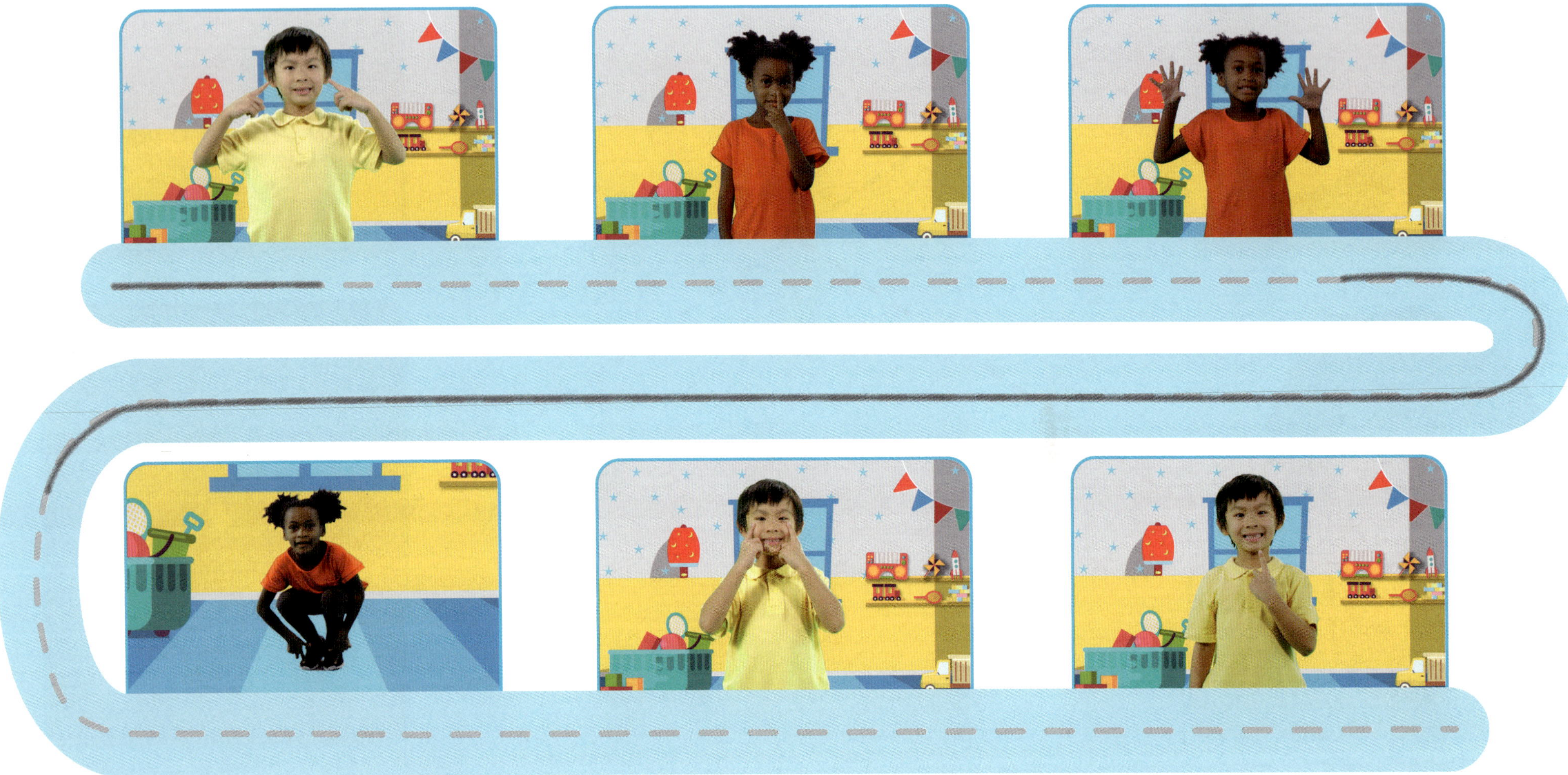

Watch. Listen, point and sing *Here are my ears*. Follow and draw a path to connect the pictures in order. Say. Language: ears, eyes, hands, mouth, nose, teeth, toes; Here is my (nose). Here are my (eyes).

Listen, point and say. Color the words you know. Stick the star sticker. Say.
Language: ears, eyes, hair, mouth, nose, teeth; I have (a mouth). I have (blue) (eyes).

Project

COOPERATIVE LEARNING

My face

Paint and decorate a face. Make a faces display. Ask and say.

Language: ears, eyes, hair, mouth, nose, teeth; boy, girl; colors; It's (a girl). I have (red) (hair). I have (green) (eyes). Where's (Maria)? Here. What color is your (nose)? It's (pink).

Clothes

Time to get dressed!

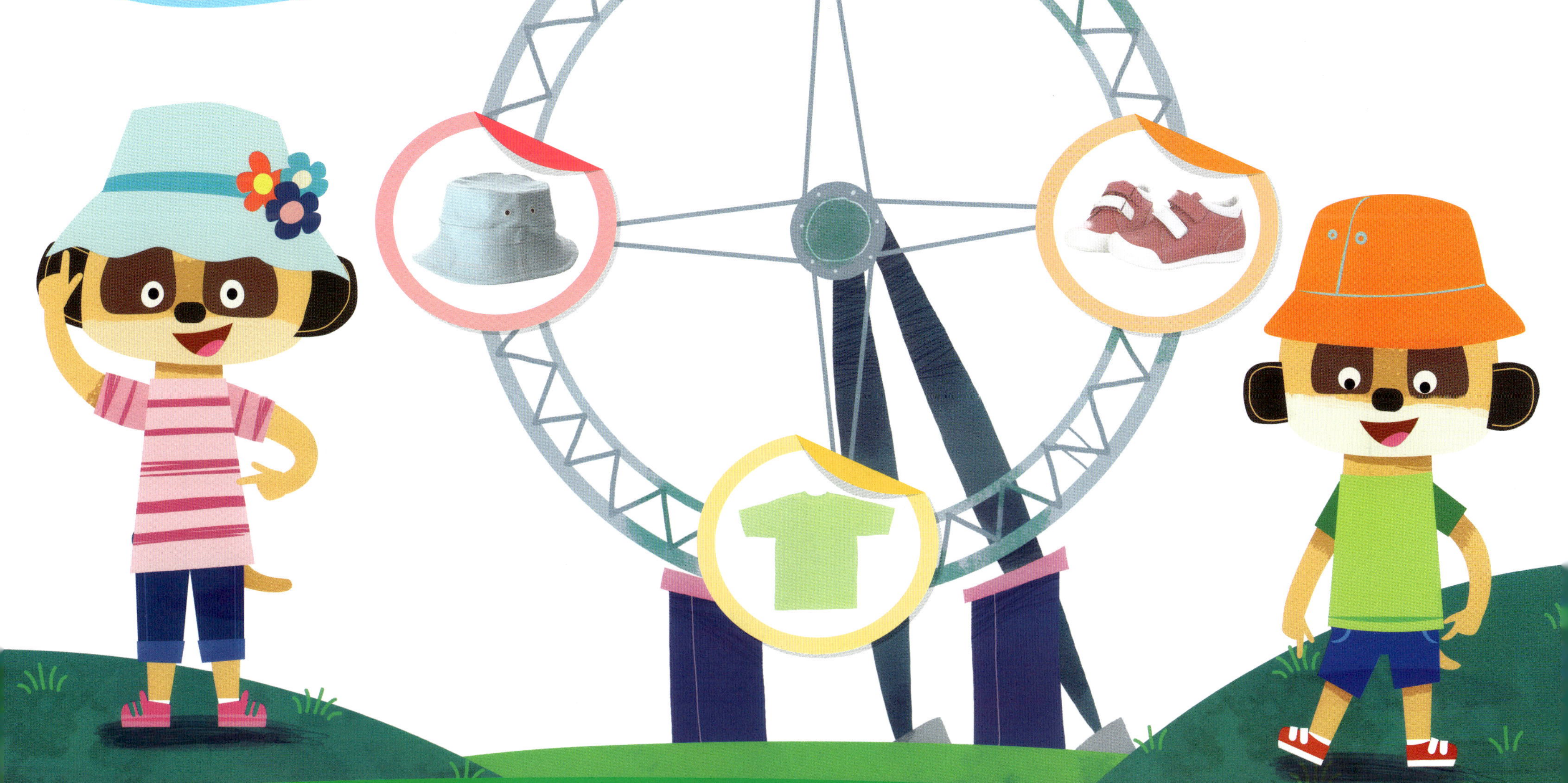

2:14 hello 2:15

Listen, point and repeat. Listen and play. Stick the clothes stickers. Say.
Language: hat, shoes, shorts, T-shirt; orange, pink, red, yellow

Language

2:16 2:17 hello

Listen and find the new clothes. Listen, point and sing *The clothes song*. Follow and draw paths to match the photos. Say.

Language: boots, coat, hat, shoes, shorts, T-shirt; Put on your (hat).

Watch. Listen to the story *Time to get dressed!* Color the trousers and hat on the monster. Stick the story sticker. Ask and say. **Language:** hat, shoes, shorts, T-shirt; Where's your (hat)? Here. Put on your (shoes). Take off your (hat).

Story Song

Watch. Listen, point and sing *Where's your T-shirt?* Color the circle to show the correct way to put on the clothes. Ask and say.

Language: hat, shoes, shorts, T-shirt; Where are your (shorts)? Here. Put on your (shoes).

Speaking

Life skills

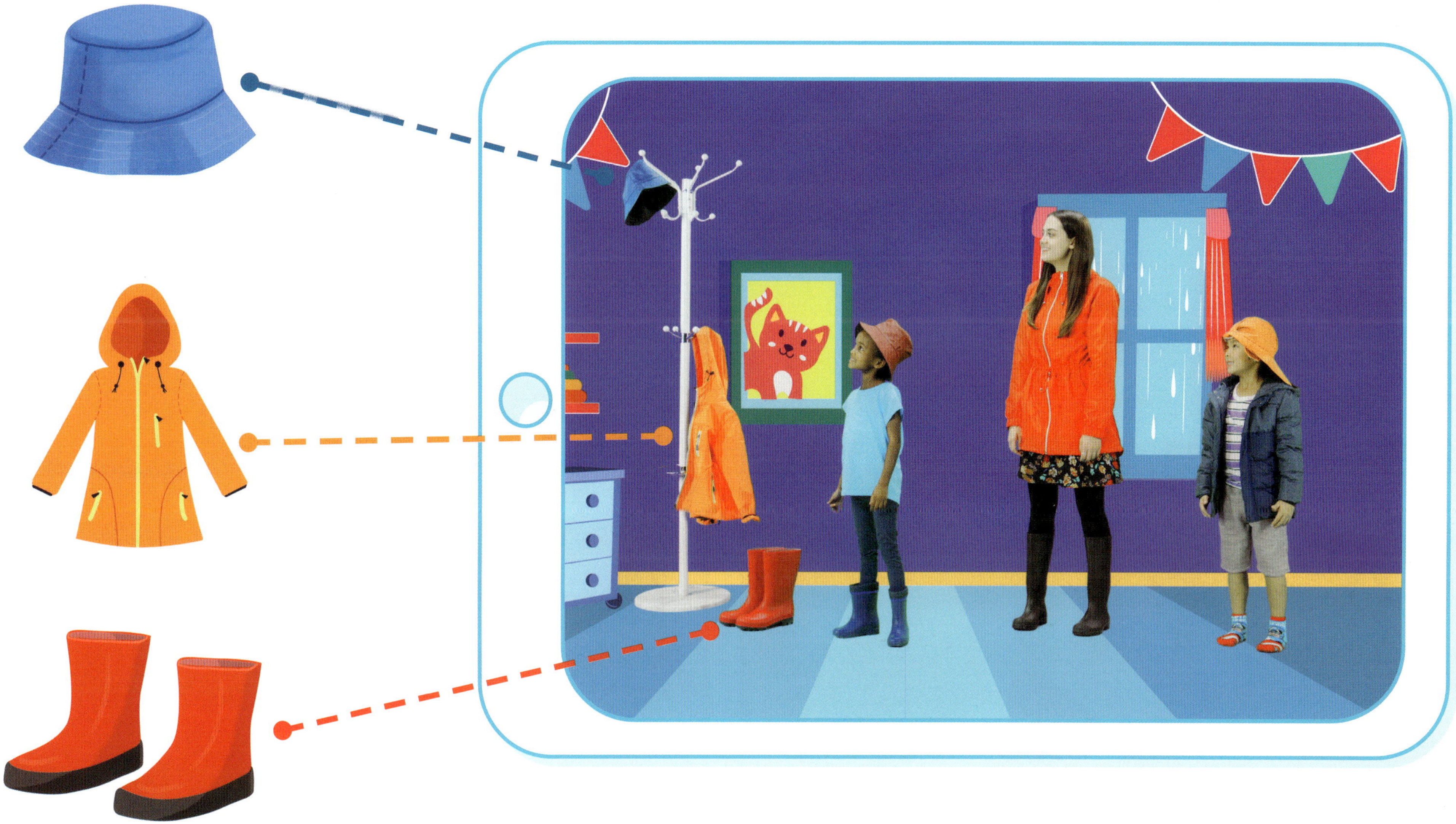

Watch. Listen and point. Trace to match Auntie Jenny's hat, Sophie's coat and Tom's boots. Ask and say. Language: boots, coat, hat; Where's your (coat)? Where are your (boots)? Here. Put on your (hat).

Listen, point and sing *I'm neat*. Color the star on the picture that shows the clothes in the correct place. Say.
Language: boots, coat, hat, shoes; neat; I'm neat. I put my (coat) away.

SOCIAL AND EMOTIONAL LEARNING

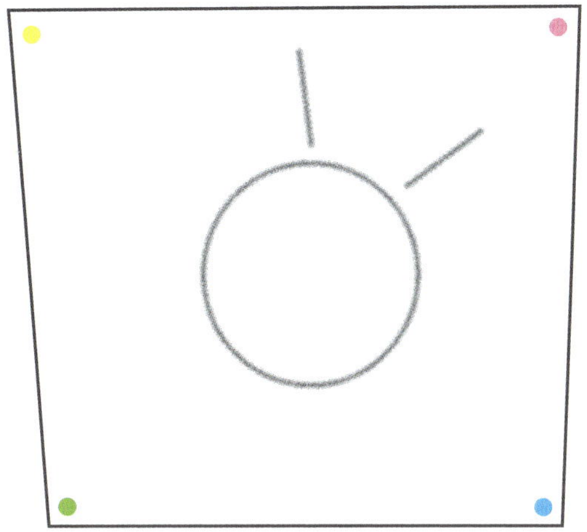

Listen and point. Draw the sunny and rainy weather in the correct place. Say.
Language: boots, coat, hat, shoes, shorts, T-shirt; rainy, sunny; It's (rainy). I put on my (coat).

Culture

Watch. Listen, point and sing *Itsy, bitsy spider*. Trace to match the pictures to the actions. Say.
Language: spider; rain, sun

Listen, point and say. Color the words you know. Stick the star sticker. Ask and say.
Language: boots, coat, hat, shoes, shorts, T-shirt; Put on your (hat). Take off your (coat). Where's your (T-shirt)? Where are your (shorts)? Here.

Project

COOPERATIVE LEARNING

Choose and paint a picture of clothes for sunny or rainy weather. Make a weather display. Ask and say. **Language:** boots, coat, hat, shoes, shorts, T-shirt; rainy, sunny; colors; It's (rainy). I put on my (coat). Where's your (hat)? Where are your (shorts)? Here. What color is your (coat)? It's (blue).

Toys

The old toy box

2:27 hello 2:28

Listen, point and repeat. Listen and play. Stick the toy stickers. Say.
Language: ball, car, doll, teddy; blue, green, orange, yellow

Listen and find the new toys. Listen, point and sing ***What's this?***
Trace to match the scooter and the train. Ask and say.
Language: ball, car, doll, scooter, teddy, train; What's this? It's (a train).

Lesson 3 Story

Watch. Listen to the story *The old toy box*. Color the teddy from the story. Stick the story sticker. Ask and say. **Language:** ball, teddy, train; What's this? It's (a train). Let's play with the (ball).

Story Song

Watch. Listen, point and sing *Let's look in the toy box.* Find and color the toys. Say.

Language: ball, teddy, train; Let's play with the (ball).

Watch. Listen and point. Trace to circle Tom's favorite toy red and Sophie's favorite toy green. Draw a picture of your favorite toy. Ask and say. Language: ball, car, doll, scooter, teddy, train; What's this? It's (my ball). What's your favorite toy? It's (my teddy).

Values We play together

Listen, point and sing *Let's play together*. Trace the mouths to show working and playing together. Say.
Language: play, work; Let's (play) together.

SOCIAL AND EMOTIONAL LEARNING

Content

2:37

hello

Listen and point. Follow and draw paths to match the activities to the places. Say.
Language: classroom, playground; play, work; I (play) in the (playground).

Culture

Watch. Listen, point and say *Bouncy ball.* Trace the line of the bouncy ball. Say.
Language: ball; big, bouncy, round; numbers 1–3

Listen, point and say. Color the words you know. Stick the star sticker. Ask and say. Language: ball, car, doll, scooter, teddy, train; What's this? It's a (train). Let's play with the (car). What's your favorite toy? It's (my doll).

Project

COOPERATIVE LEARNING

Choose, paint and decorate a toy. Make a toy mobile. Ask and say.
Language: ball, doll, teddy, train; colors; What's this? It's (a teddy). Let's play with the (ball). Where's the (red) (train)? Here. What's your favorite toy? It's (the teddy).

Food
The picnic

Listen, point and repeat. Listen and play. Stick the food stickers. Say.
Language: apple, banana, cookie, sandwich; blue, green, pink, red

Language

3:03

3:04

hello

Listen and find the new food. Listen, point and sing *I like bananas*. Color the faces and trace to match them to the water and the juice. Point and say.
Language: apples, bananas, cookies, juice, sandwiches, water; I like (bananas).

Story

3:06

hello

Watch. Listen to the story *The picnic*. Trace to circle the picnic lunch in the story. Stick the story sticker. Ask and say. Language: banana, cookie, juice, sandwich; I'm hungry. Can I have my lunch, please? Here's (a sandwich) for you. Thank you. I like (bananas).

Story Song

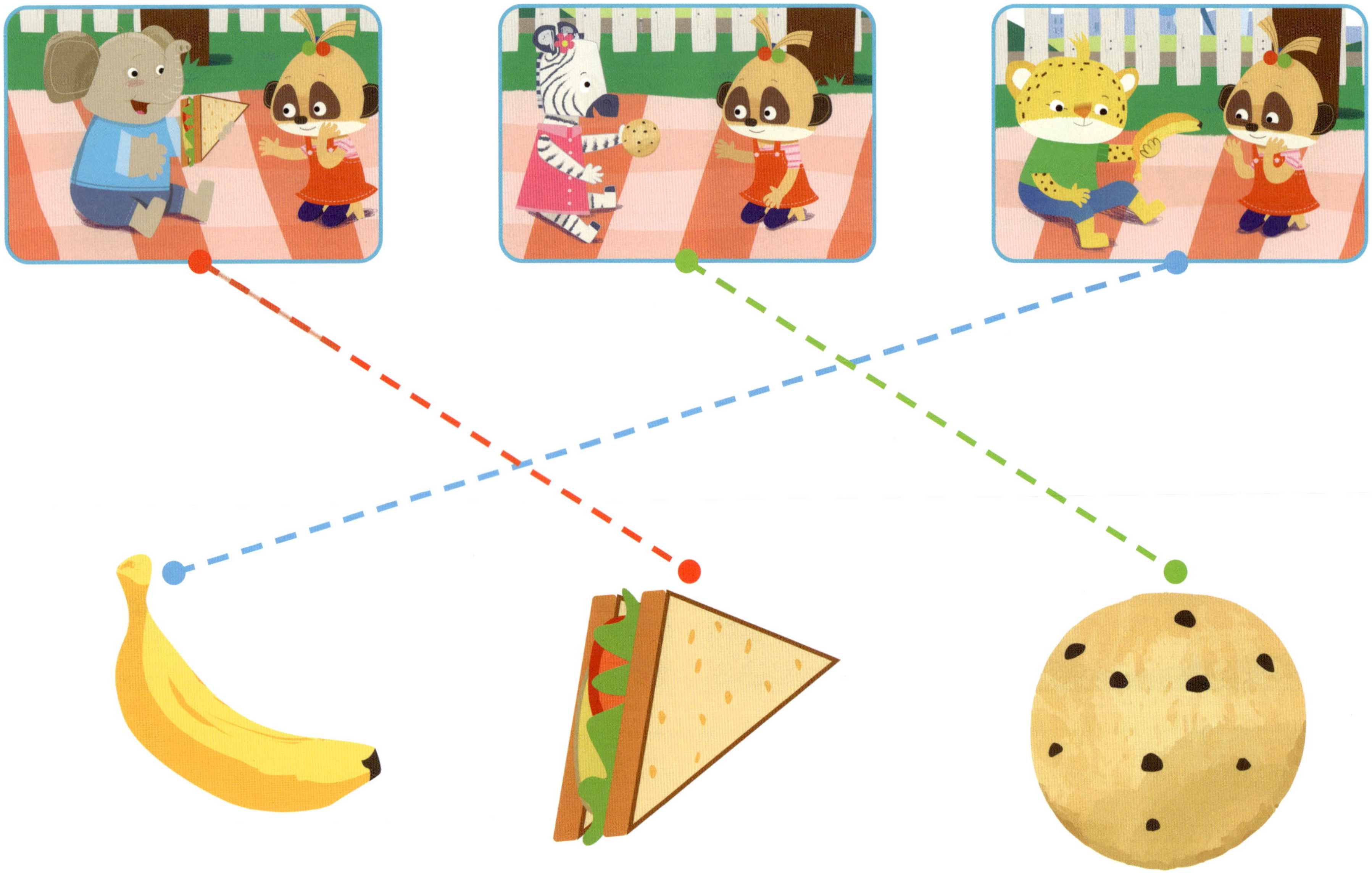

Watch. Listen, point and sing *I'm hungry*. Trace to match the characters to the food they give Mimi. Point and say. Language: banana, cookie, sandwich; I'm hungry. Here's (a sandwich) for you. Thank you.

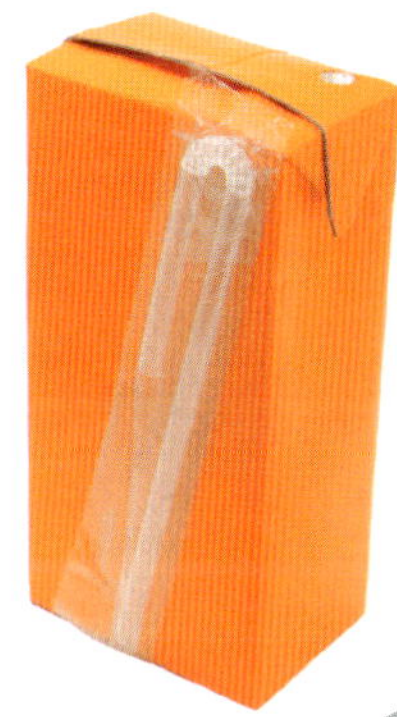

Watch. Listen and point. Trace to circle what Sophie asks for in red and what Tom asks for in blue. Ask and say. **Language:** banana, juice, sandwich, water; Are you hungry? Can I have (a sandwich), please? Here you go. Thank you. I like (bananas).

Values I say 'please' and 'thank you'

Listen, point and sing *Two little words*. Color the star yellow for 'please' and pink for 'thank you'. Say.

Language: please, thank you

3:10

hello

SOCIAL AND EMOTIONAL LEARNING

Content

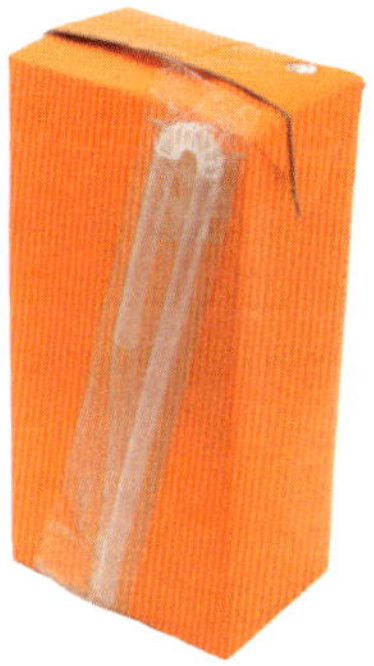

Listen and point. Color the circles green to show what we eat and blue to show what we drink. Say. Language: drink, eat; apples, bananas, cookies, juice, sandwiches, water; I eat (cookies). I drink (water).

Culture

Watch. Listen, point and sing *Ten little apples*. Color and count the apples and oranges. Say.

Language: apple, orange; little; tree; numbers 1–10

Review

Listen, point and say. Color the words you know. Stick the star sticker. Ask and say.
Language: apple, banana, cookie, juice, sandwich, water; I'm hungry. Are you hungry? Can I have (a cookie), please? Here you go. Here's (a banana) for you. Thank you. I like (sandwiches).

Project

COOPERATIVE LEARNING

1

2

3

Make food you like for a picnic. Paint a picnic blanket. Make a picnic display. Ask and say.
Language: apple, banana, cookie, juice, sandwich, water; I'm hungry. Are you hungry? Can I have (a cookie), please? Here you go. Here's (a cookie) for you. Thank you. I like (sandwiches). What color is the (apple)? It's (green).

Pets
The little dog

Vocabulary Lesson 1

3:14 hello 3:15

Listen, point and repeat. Listen and play. Stick the pet stickers. Say.
Language: bird, fish, mouse, rabbit; orange, pink, red, yellow

Lesson 2 Language

Listen and find the new pets. Listen, point and sing *I have a cat*.
Trace to match the cat and the dog. Say.
Language: bird, cat, dog, fish, mouse, rabbit; I have a (mouse).

Story

3:19

hello

Watch. Listen to the story *The little dog*. Trace to circle the animal in the story. Stick the story sticker. Ask and say. Language: cat, dog, rabbit; mommy; happy, sad; Is this your mommy? Yes, it is. / No, it isn't. It's (a rabbit). I'm (happy).

Story Song

Watch. Listen, point and sing *I'm a little dog*. Color the little dog's mommy. Ask and say.
Language: cat, dog, rabbit; mommy; happy, sad; Is this your mommy? Yes, it is. / No, it isn't.
It's (a rabbit). I'm (happy).

Lesson 5 Speaking

Life skills

Watch. Listen and point. Color the circles to show the colors of Sophie and Tom's pets. Ask and say. Language: bird, fish; blue, orange; I have (a bird). Is this your (fish)? Yes, it is. / No, it isn't. This is my (fish). My fish is (orange).

Values I'm kind to you

Listen, point and sing *I'm kind to you*. Color the faces to show how you're kind. Say.

Language: I'm kind to you. I help you.

SOCIAL AND EMOTIONAL LEARNING

Content

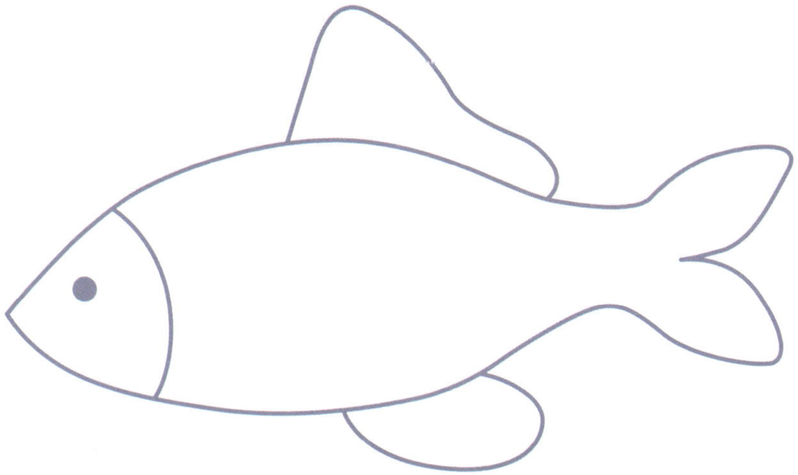

Listen and point. Color the animal that flies red. Color the animal that swims green. Say. Language: fly, swim; birds, fish; Birds fly. Fish swim.

Culture

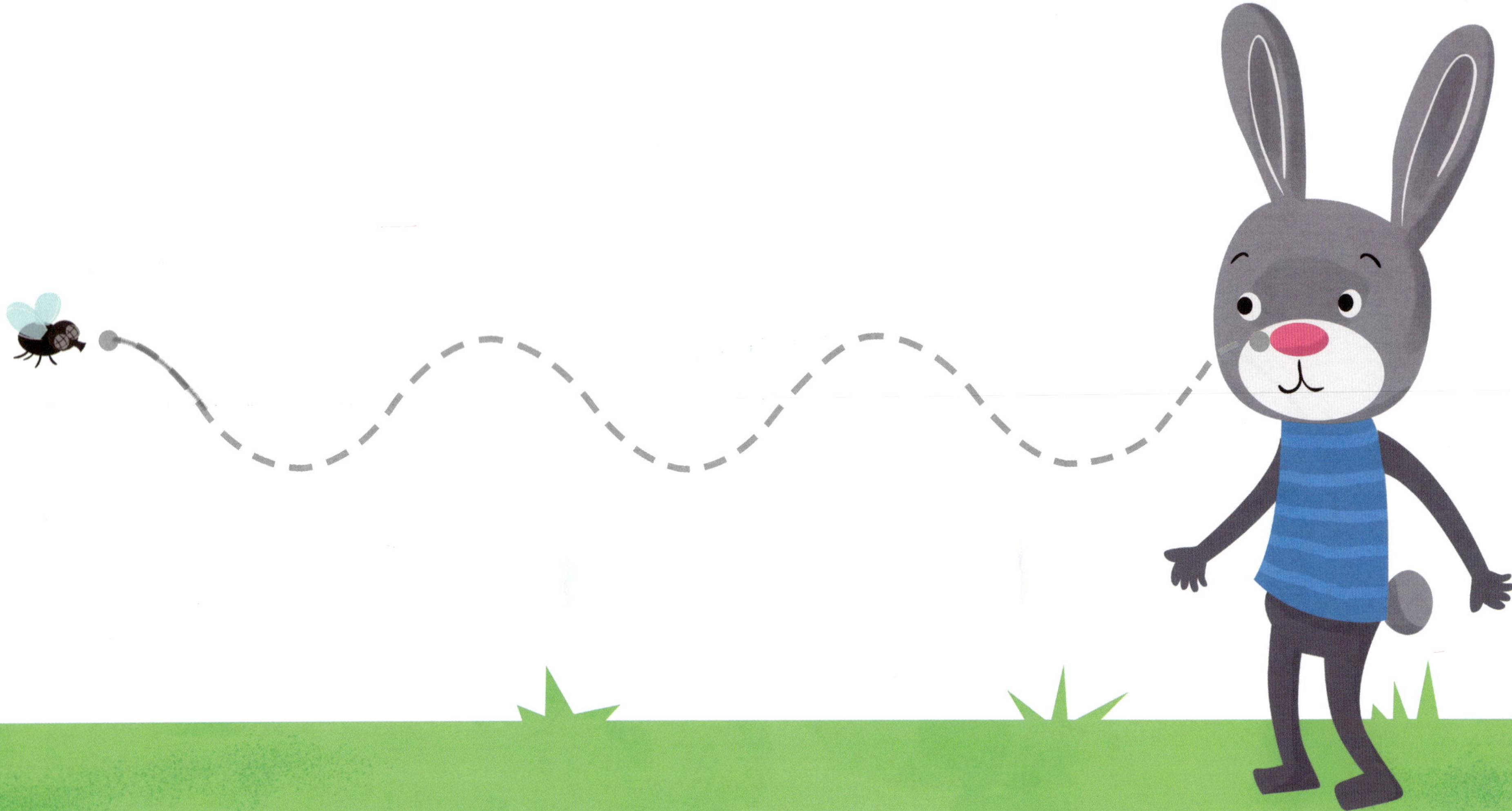

Watch. Listen, point and sing *Little Peter Rabbit*. Trace the line of the fly to Peter Rabbit's nose. Say. **Language:** fly, rabbit; nose; little; Little Peter Rabbit has a fly on his nose.

Listen, point and say. Color the words you know. Stick the star sticker. Ask and say. Language: bird, cat, dog, fish, mouse, rabbit; I have (a mouse). Is this your (cat)? Yes, it is. / No, it isn't. This is my (mouse).

COOPERATIVE LEARNING

1

2

3

Paint and decorate your favorite pet. Make a poster of your favorite pets. Ask and say.

Language: cat, dog, fish, rabbit; colors; Is this your (cat)? Yes, it is. / No, it isn't. I have (a dog). What's this? It's (a cat). Where's the (yellow) (rabbit)? Here. This is my (fish). What color is your (fish)? It's (orange).

Beach

Five little crabs

3:27 hello 3:28

Listen, point and repeat. Listen and play. Stick the beach stickers. Say.

Language: crab, ocean, sand, shell; blue, green, orange, yellow

Listen and find the new beach words. Listen, point and sing *I can see the ocean*. Match the photos to the picture. Say.
Language: bucket, crab, ocean, sand, shell, shovel; I can see (a crab). Me too.

Story

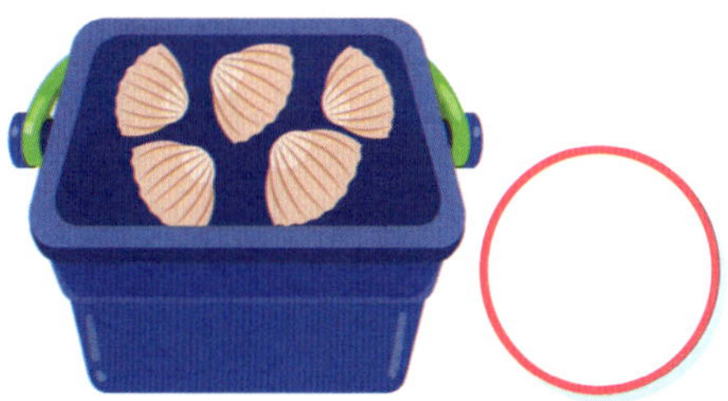

Watch. Listen to the story *Five little crabs*. Color the circle next to the bucket in the story. Stick the story sticker. Ask and say. **Language:** bucket, crab, ocean, sand, shovel; numbers 1–5; little; I can see (five) little crabs. Me too. How many little crabs? (Five).

Story Song

Watch. Listen, point and sing *One, two, three, four, five little crabs.*
Color and count the crabs. Ask and say.
Language: bucket, crab, ocean; little; numbers 1–5; How many little crabs? (Five).

Watch. Listen and point. Trace to circle the number of shells in Tom and Sophie's buckets. Ask and say. Language: bucket, ocean, sand, shell; pink; numbers 1–5; I can see (shells). How many (shells)? (Four). What color are the (shells)? They're (pink).

Listen, point and sing *I love our world*. Color the ocean blue and the trees green. Say.
Language: ocean, trees; blue, green; I love the (blue) (ocean).

Listen and point. Match the animals to where they live. Say.

Language: land, water; cat, crab, fish; (Fish) live in (water). (Cats) live on (land).

Lesson 8 **Culture**

Beach

Watch. Listen, point and sing *One, two, three, four, five.*
Trace to circle the animals in the song. Point and say.
Language: crab, fish, shell; numbers 1–10

Review

Beach

Listen, point and say. Color the words you know. Stick the star sticker. Ask and say.
Language: bucket, crab, ocean, sand, shell, shovel; numbers 1–3; colors; I can see (a bucket). Me too. How many (shells)? (Three). What color are the (shells)? They're (pink).

Project

COOPERATIVE LEARNING

1

2

3

Paint and decorate an object from the beach. Make a beach display. Ask and say. Language: bucket, crab, ocean, sand, shell, shovel; colors; numbers; I can see (a shell). Me too. How many (crabs)? (Five). Is this your (bucket)? Yes, it is. / No, it isn't. I have (a shovel). What's this? It's (a crab). Where's the (green) (bucket)? Here.

Colors

Listen, point and say. Color the balls so they are the same.
Language: blue, green, red, yellow

Colors

Listen, point and say. Color the butterfly so the wings are the same.
Language: brown, orange, pink, purple

Numbers 1 2 3 4 5

1 2 3 4 5

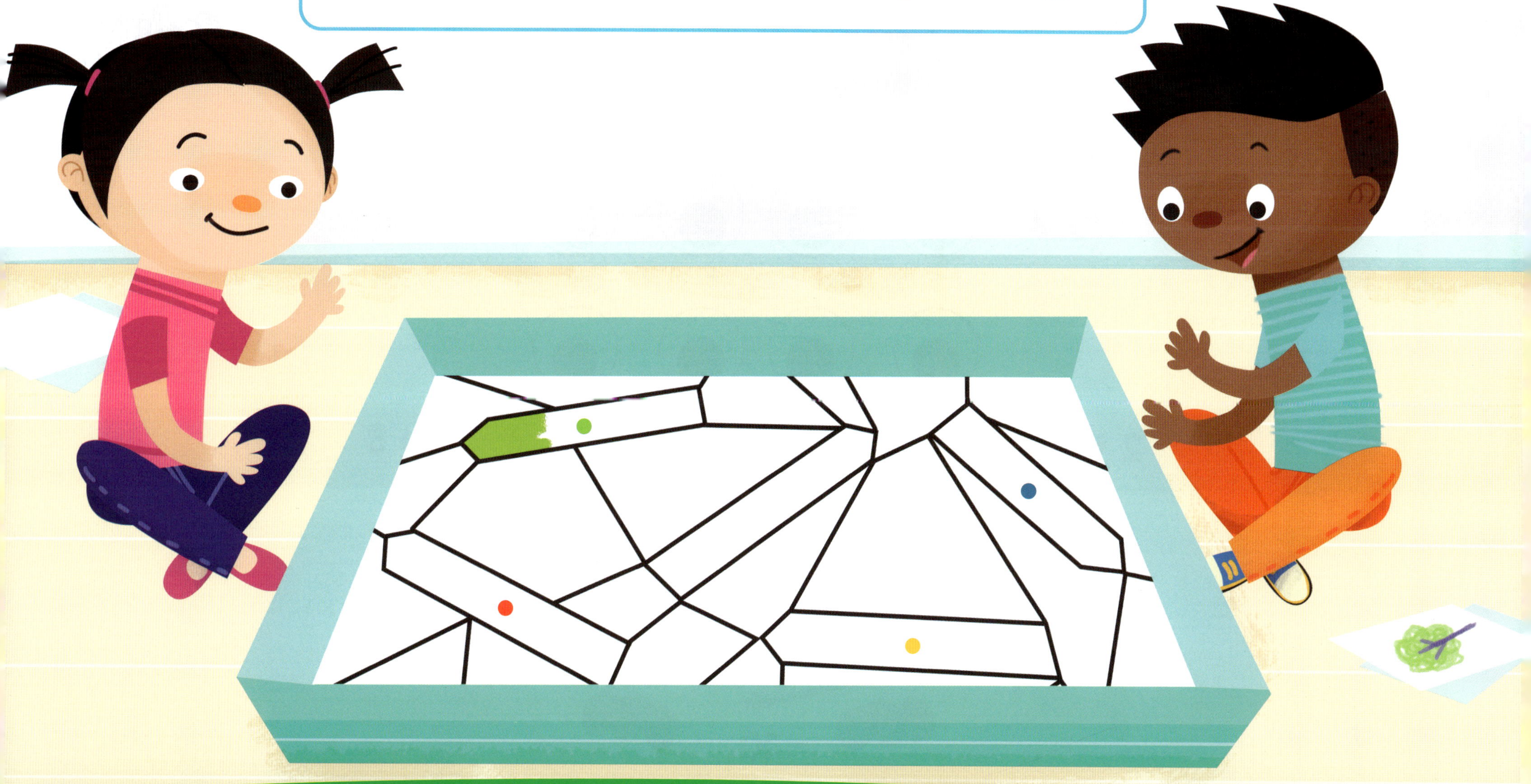

Listen, point and say. Color and count the crayons. Circle the correct number.
Language: one, two, three, four, five

Numbers 1 2 3 4 5 6 7 8 9 10

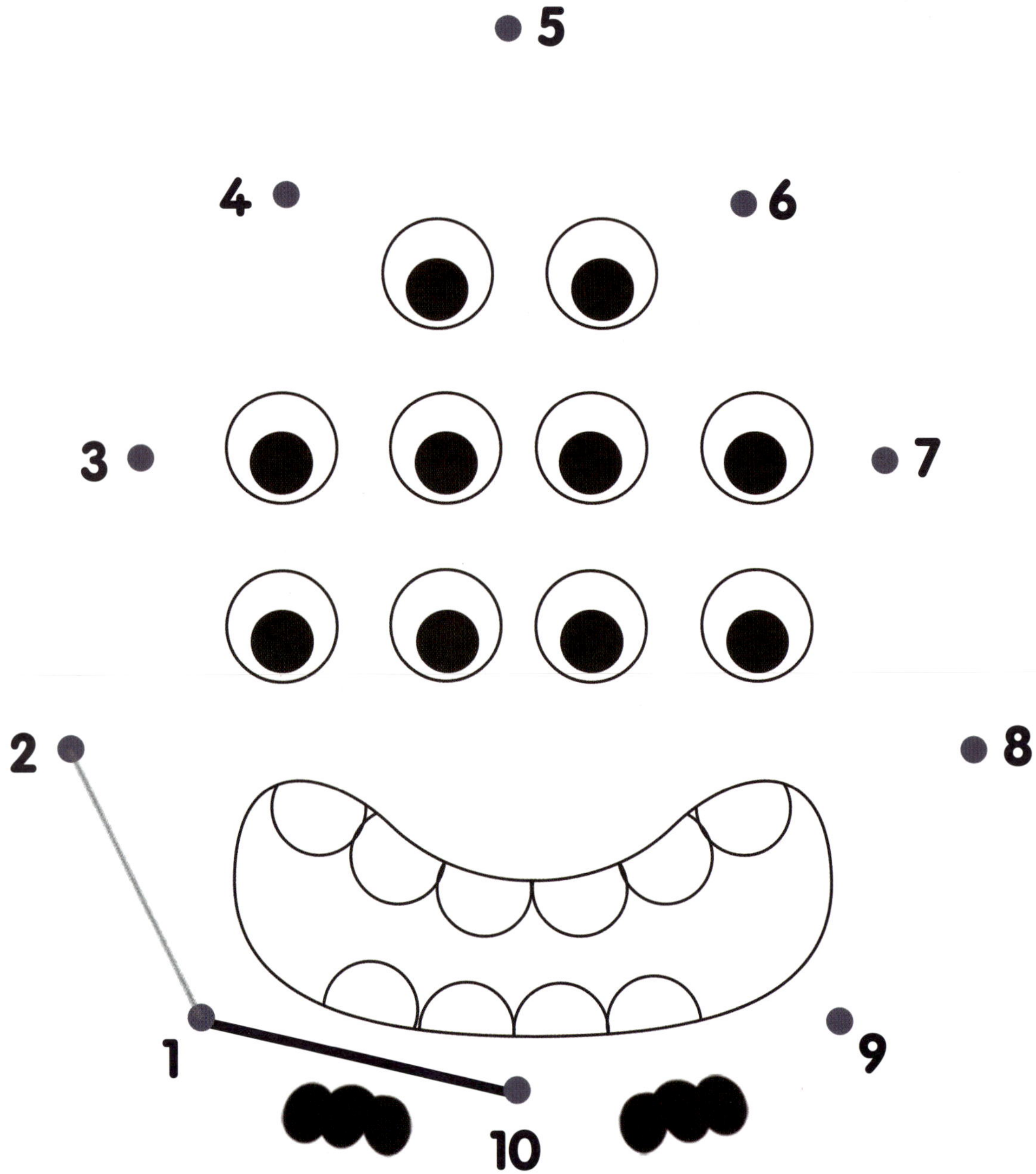

Listen, point and say. Connect the dots. Color the monster.
Count the eyes and teeth.
Language: numbers 1–10

Shapes

Listen, point and say. Trace the circles and triangles.
Language: circle, triangle

Shapes

Listen, point and say. Trace and color the squares red and the rectangles blue.
Language: square, rectangle

Concepts

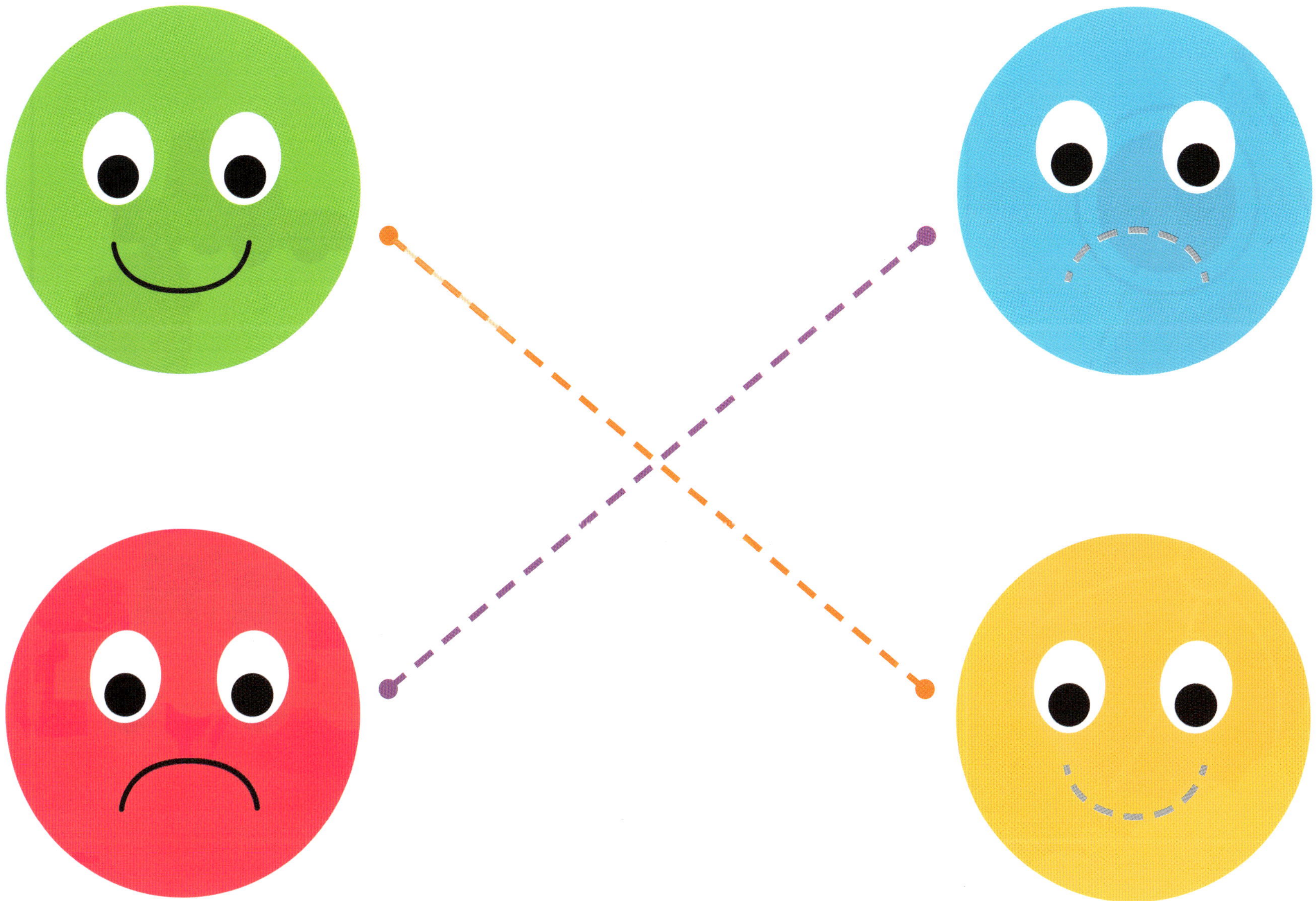

Listen, point and say. Trace to match the happy faces and the sad faces. Trace the mouths.
Language: happy, sad

Festivals

Carnival

Listen, point and say. Listen and sing *Carnival parade*. Color and count the Carnival masks.
Language: Carnival, mask, parade; dance, sing; numbers 1–5

Festivals

International Family Day

Listen, point and say. Listen and sing *Happy Family Day*. Draw a picture of your family. Language: happy, family; mommy, daddy, grandma, grandpa, brother, sister

Festivals

Teddy Bear Day

Listen, point and say. Listen and sing *I love my teddy bear*. Trace and color the teddy bears. Color the circle of the teddy bear you like.
Language: brown; eyes, feet, fur; teddy bear

Hello

Family

Classroom

My face

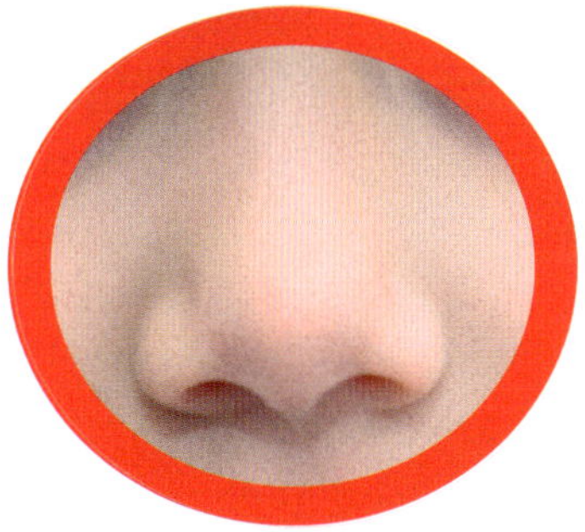
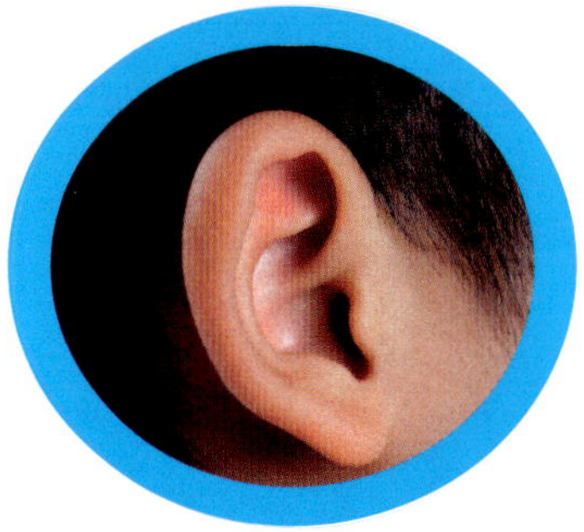
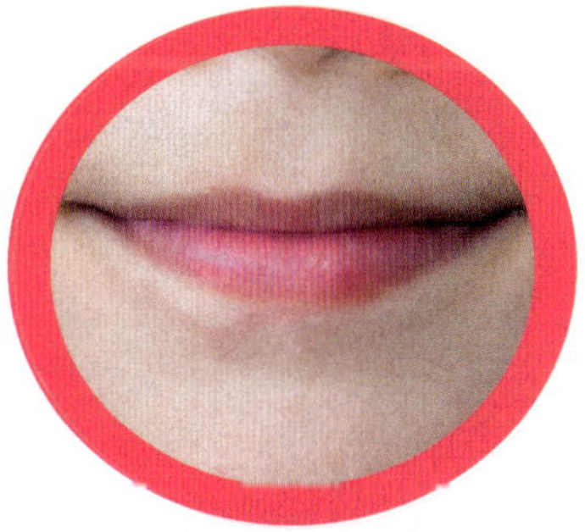
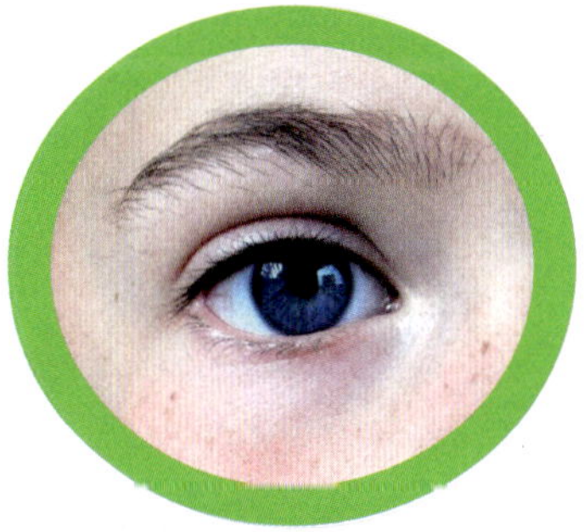

Clothes

Toys

Food

Pets

Beach